# MEDICAL JUDICIAL RELEASE
## *in Ohio*

*A step-by-step petition playbook for securing early release from incarceration on grounds of medical necessity.*

**SECOND OHIO LEGAL PUBLISHING COMPANY**
A division of LegalOwl216 LLC · Cleveland, Ohio

## Medical Judicial Release in Ohio

First Edition · June 2026



Published by Second Ohio Legal Publishing Company, a division of LegalOwl216 LLC, Cleveland, Ohio.



**Disclaimer:** This book is an educational and procedural reference. It is not legal advice, and reading or using it does not create an attorney-client relationship. Statutes, administrative rules, agency policies, and earned-credit provisions change over time; verify every authority against the current official source before relying on it. Anyone facing an actual proceeding should retain a licensed Ohio attorney.



**ISBN:** [ ISBN to be assigned ]

Printed in the United States of America.

# Contents

---


**PART I · Understanding Medical Judicial Release**

Important Notice 1
How to Use This Playbook 2
1. The Big Picture 3
2. Eligibility and Legal Framework 4
3. The Five-Phase Process Map 6
4. Stakeholder Directory 10
5. Evidence and Documentation Checklist 11
6. Drafting the Motion 12
7. Community Re-Entry and the Managed Care Transition Plan 14
8. Fallback Strategies ("Plan B") 15
9. Attorney–Client Access and Inmate Legal Rights 17

**PART II · The Toolkit: Templates & Worksheets**

Sample Motion for Medical Judicial Release 21
Sample Proposed Order 23
Sample Certificate Request Letter to the Health Care Administrator 24
Worksheet 1: Case Intake and Representation 27
Worksheet 2: Records and Documents Collection 28
Worksheet 3: Medical Threshold Eligibility 29
Worksheet 4: Five-Phase Progress Tracker 30
Worksheet 5: Stakeholder Contact Log 31
Worksheet 6: Community Re-Entry & MCTP Planning 32
Worksheet 7: Evidence and Exhibit Index 33
Worksheet 8: Hearing Preparation Checklist 34
Worksheet 9: Fallback Strategy Decision Guide 35
Worksheet 10: Cost & Logistics Planner 36
Care & Placement Readiness 37
What Goes in Your Case Binder 38
Questions to Ask Your Attorney 39
Phase Action Pages 40
Motion Drafting Pages 45
Meeting & Call Notes 50

**PART III · Reference & Support**

Glossary of Key Terms 57
Frequently Asked Questions 59
Resources and Where to Find Help 60
Appendix A — Key Authorities Quick-Reference 61
Appendix B — Template Field Glossary 62
Appendix C — Master Checklist 63
Notes 64

PART I

# Understanding Medical Judicial Release

*What the process is, who decides, and how the pieces fit together.*

## Important Notice

> **Educational use only — not legal advice.**
> This playbook is an educational and procedural reference. It does not constitute legal advice, and reading or using it does not create an attorney-client relationship. Medical judicial release turns on the specific facts of an individual case, the current text of Ohio statutes and administrative rules, and the discretion of the sentencing court. Anyone facing an actual proceeding should retain a licensed Ohio attorney.

**Currency of the law.** Ohio Revised Code provisions, Administrative Code rules, ODRC policies, and earned-credit caps cited here change over time through legislation and rulemaking. Verify every authority against the current official source before relying on it.

**Template fields.** Bracketed and generic placeholders — such as "Incarcerated Person," "ABC Correctional Institution," "ABC County," "Neighboring County," "[Inmate #]," and "[Month, Day, Year]" — mark information that must be supplied for a specific matter. Appendix B lists each field.

**Scope.** The playbook addresses the adult Ohio system administered by the Ohio Department of Rehabilitation and Correction (ODRC) and proceedings in the Ohio Courts of Common Pleas. It does not cover federal custody or other states.

# How to Use This Playbook

This playbook consolidates the medical judicial release process into one working reference. It is written for a mixed audience, so the legal framework and the human steps sit side by side.

### Two ways to read it

**Attorneys and advocates** will find the controlling authorities, the stakeholder chain, the evidentiary anchor, the motion framework, and the fallback strategies in Sections 2, 4, 6, and 8, with a quick-reference authorities table in Appendix A.

**Families, caregivers, and supporters** will find the plain-language summaries at the start of each section, the five-phase process map in Section 3, the re-entry planning steps in Section 7, and the master checklist in Appendix C the most useful starting points.

> **How the cues work**
> **Plain language** boxes translate a section into everyday terms.
> **Practice pointer** boxes flag the moves that most often decide whether a petition succeeds.

# 1. The Big Picture

**Plain language**

Some people in Ohio prisons become so sick that keeping them locked up no longer protects anyone. Ohio law lets them ask to be released early so they can get care in the community. The strongest version of this request goes to the judge who originally sentenced the person, and the judge decides. This playbook walks through how that request is built and granted.

## Two paths to medical early release

Ohio offers more than one route to early release on medical grounds, but they are not equal in practice.

**Path 1 — Judicial Medical Release (the focus of this playbook).** Decided by the sentencing judge in the County Court of Common Pleas under the judicial release framework and ODRC Policy 66-ILL-01 / OCHC Protocol B-35. The court holds ultimate discretion. This path keeps the decision with a local judge rather than the Parole Board or the Governor, and ODRC policy itself encourages routing medical-release decisions to the sentencing court.

**Path 2 — Administrative "release as if on parole."** An executive mechanism that is frequently unavailable here: it is barred where the incarcerated person is serving a mandatory sentence for an offense of violence. Because the model case involves a Robbery (F2) offense of violence and a mandatory term, this path is generally foreclosed, which is precisely why the judicial path matters.

**Practice pointer**

Lead with the judicial path. The judge's discretion is the opening that the mandatory-sentence and offense-of-violence rules tend to close on the administrative side. Everything in this playbook is built to put a complete, court-ready record in front of that judge.

# 2. Eligibility and Legal Framework

**Plain language**

To qualify, a doctor inside the prison must certify that the person is gravely ill in one of three specific ways. There is also a major obstacle: a mandatory sentence for a violent crime blocks the easier administrative route. The judge, however, can still grant release on the judicial path.

## The three medical thresholds

Under ODRC Policy 66-ILL-01, the incarcerated person's condition must satisfy at least one of the following definitions. Meeting any one of the three opens the door to consideration.

| Threshold | Definition |
|---|---|
| Terminally ill | An irreversible, incurable condition likely to cause death within twelve months. |
| Imminent danger of death | A condition with a reasonably low probability of survival beyond six months. |
| Medically incapacitated | A diagnosable condition that prevents the person from completing activities of daily living (ADLs) without continuous medical care, to the point that continued institutional security is unnecessary. |

## The offense-of-violence and mandatory-sentence hurdle

An individual is **ineligible** for administrative "release as if on parole" while serving a mandatory prison term for an offense of violence. In the model case, the Robbery (F2) conviction is an offense of violence and the neighboring-county docket carries a mandatory two-year term. Standard, non-medical judicial release is also out of reach in the near term: under *State v. Clinkscale*, where a sentence includes a mandatory prison term, the offender must fully serve that mandatory time before any waiting period even begins, and jail-time credit cannot shorten that waiting period.

**Why the judicial medical path survives this.** The medical judicial release route places ultimate discretion with the sentencing judge rather than the Parole Board or Governor. ODRC Legal Services will still scrutinize statutory eligibility closely once the medical certificate issues, so the medical evidence must be meticulously prepared to persuade the court.

## Key authorities at a glance

| Authority | What it governs |
|---|---|
| ORC § 2929.20 | Judicial release — the statutory vehicle for an early-release motion before the sentencing court. |

| Authority | What it governs |
|---|---|
| ODRC Policy 66-ILL-01 | Defines the three medical thresholds and encourages medical-release decisions by local sentencing courts. |
| OCHC Protocol B-35 | The Office of Correctional Health Care protocol that initiates a medical release evaluation at the facility. |
| OAC 5120-9-17 | Administrative-code basis ODRC Legal Services uses to confirm medical-release eligibility. |
| ORC § 2967.05 | Administrative "medical release as if on parole" — the path generally barred by a mandatory violent-offense term. |
| ORC § 2967.271 (Reagan Tokes / SB 201) | Presumptive release at the minimum term and the Director's exceptional-conduct reduction (see Section 8). |

*See Appendix A for the full authorities quick-reference.*

# 3. The Five-Phase Process Map

**Plain language**

From start to finish, a medical judicial release moves through five stages: hire a lawyer and gather records; get the prison doctor to certify the illness; build a plan for care at home; pass the state's investigation and get the ODRC Director's recommendation; and finally have the judge hold a hearing and decide.

## Phase 1 — Legal Retention and Case Initiation

| Owner | Key task | Notes |
|---|---|---|
| Client / representative & Attorney | Execute the representation agreement | Both attorney and client sign a written agreement establishing representation specifically for a "Motion for Hearing for Judicial Order for Early Release from Incarceration on Grounds of Medical Necessity." |
| Client / representative | Strict adherence to no-contact rules | The incarcerated person and their representative must not contact any witnesses or alleged victims (for example, an assaulted peace officer) under any circumstances. |
| Client / representative | Document provision | Promptly provide all requested documents to the attorney, including birth certificate, Social Security card, and any medical or housing documentation needed for the re-entry plan. |

## Phase 2 — Medical Certification (Institutional Level)

| Owner | Key task | Notes |
|---|---|---|
| Health Care Administrator (HCA) | Initiate the protocol | The attorney formally requests that the facility HCA initiate a medical release evaluation via |

| Owner | Key task | Notes |
|---|---|---|
| | | OCHC Protocol B-35. |
| Chief Medical Officer (CMO) | Conduct the medical evaluation | Evaluate whether the person has become medically incapacitated, terminally ill, or in imminent danger of death. |
| Chief Medical Officer (CMO) | Issue the CMO certificate | Issue the official certificate stating the diagnosis, ambulatory status, prognosis (e.g., survival probability under six months), the minimum community placement required, and the medical category. |
| HCA → ODRC Legal Services | Route the certificate | The HCA sends the completed CMO certificate to the ODRC Legal Services counsel assigned to the Office of Correctional Health Care. |

> **Practice pointer**
> The CMO certificate is the evidentiary anchor of the entire petition. Phase 2 is where most matters stall, so press the HCA — in writing, on firm letterhead — to prompt the CMO to issue it. Nothing downstream can carry the motion without it.

## Phase 3 — Community Re-Entry Planning

| Owner | Key task | Notes |
|---|---|---|
| Client / IMPC | Medicaid pre-release enrollment | The person works directly with the Institution Medicaid Program Coordinator (IMPC) to complete the Medicaid application before release so community care is funded. |
| Client supporter / CLW | Establish the managed care transition plan | Meet with the Release Planning Coordinator and the prison's Community Linkage Worker (CLW), |

| Owner | Key task | Notes |
| --- | --- | --- |
| | | who schedules the first community physical and behavioral-health appointments so there is no lapse in care. |
| Client supporter | Prepare the housing environment | Ensure the home accommodates the person's activities of daily living (ADLs) and secure stable housing, which the state weighs heavily. |
| Client supporter | Finalize the transportation plan | Establish and document the exact arrangements for transporting the person from the prison to the home on release day. |

## Phase 4 — ODRC Administrative Investigation and Director Approval

| Owner | Key task | Notes |
| --- | --- | --- |
| ODRC Legal Services | Legal clearance | Review the CMO certificate, confirm statutory eligibility, and forward the file to the Division of Parole and Community Services (DPCS). |
| DPCS Deputy Director | Placement Investigation Request (PIR) | Initiate a detailed investigation; DPCS field staff investigate the supporter's home to confirm it is an appropriate community placement. |
| DPCS | Compile the investigation dossier | Gather the Warden's Institutional Summary Report (ISR) on conduct, verify the transportation plan, and solicit input from the sentencing court, county prosecutor, and Office of Victim Services (OVS). |
| ODRC Director | Director's certification | Review the completed |

| Owner | Key task | Notes |
| --- | --- | --- |
| | | investigation and CMO certificate, formally recommend the medical judicial release, and forward the certification to the sentencing court. |

## Phase 5 — Judicial Proceedings

| Owner | Key task | Notes |
| --- | --- | --- |
| Defense counsel | File the motion | File the Motion for Medical Judicial Release in the County Court of Common Pleas, attaching the CMO certificate, the Director's recommendation, and the community re-entry plan. |
| Court & County Prosecutor | Statutory notifications & opposition | The court and prosecutor notify the victims (including any peace officer). The prosecutor and victims may submit statements or testimony opposing release based on the nature of the offenses. |
| Sentencing judge | Judicial determination | Review the briefs, medical evidence, and opposition. The judge exercises total discretion to grant or deny the release. |
| Adult Parole Authority (APA) | Post-release control (if granted) | If granted, the person is transferred to the supporter's care and placed under APA supervision subject to community-control sanctions set by the court. |

# 4. Stakeholder Directory

A medical judicial release requires navigating a network of medical, administrative, and judicial actors. This directory consolidates who does what across all five phases.

| Stakeholder | Role in the process |
|---|---|
| Health Care Administrator (HCA) | Monitors the medical condition and coordinates with Legal Services to initiate the OCHC Protocol B-35 evaluation. |
| Chief Medical Officer (CMO) | The linchpin. Issues the formal medical certificate documenting diagnosis, prognosis, ambulatory status, and required care level. |
| ODRC Legal Services | Reviews the certificate and inmate file, confirms statutory eligibility (OAC 5120-9-17), and forwards the file to DPCS. |
| Warden (Managing Officer) | Formalizes the institutional recommendation and generates the Institutional Summary Report (ISR) on conduct and rehabilitation. |
| Division of Parole and Community Services (DPCS) | Conducts the placement investigation, verifies transportation, and gathers court, prosecutor, and victim input. |
| DPCS Deputy Director | Initiates the Placement Investigation Request and endorses the file upward. |
| ODRC Director | Reviews the investigation and certifies the recommendation for release to the sentencing court. |
| Sentencing Judge | Holds total discretion to grant or deny the medical judicial release. |
| County Prosecutor | Receives notice, alerts victims, and may oppose the release. |
| Victims / Office of Victim Services (OVS) | Receive notice and may submit statements or testimony; may access the ISR. |
| Institution Medicaid Program Coordinator (IMPC) | Assists with pre-release Medicaid enrollment so community care is funded. |
| Community Linkage Worker (CLW) | Schedules initial community physical and behavioral-health appointments to prevent a lapse in care. |
| Adult Parole Authority (APA) | Supervises the person post-release under court-imposed community-control sanctions. |
| Court Investigative Services / Probation | Finalizes the judicial-release report and jail-time-credit records; sets the post-release supervision level. |

# 5. Evidence and Documentation Checklist

> **Practice pointer**
> If a single document is missing, it is almost always the CMO certificate — and without it the motion cannot proceed. Build the rest of the file in parallel so that the moment the certificate issues, the motion is ready to file.

### Core evidentiary record

- ☐ **CMO medical certificate** — diagnosis, prognosis, ambulatory status, required care level, medical category, minimum community placement. (The anchor.)
- ☐ Institutional Summary Report (ISR) from the Warden — disciplinary history and rehabilitative efforts.
- ☐ ODRC Director's recommendation / certification to the sentencing court.
- ☐ DPCS placement investigation results, including the home assessment.

### Community re-entry record

- ☐ Managed Care Transition Plan (MCTP) — medical, mental-health, and recovery appointments (see Section 7).
- ☐ Proof of pre-release Medicaid enrollment.
- ☐ Written transportation plan for release day.
- ☐ Housing and ADL accommodation documentation; proof of stable housing.

### Client identity and intake

- ☐ Signed representation agreement specific to the medical-necessity motion.
- ☐ Birth certificate and Social Security card.
- ☐ Any medical or housing documentation requested by counsel.

# 6. Drafting the Motion

*Motion Framework — **State v. [Incarcerated Person]**. Use the following six-part outline to assemble a court-ready motion for medical judicial release.*

### I. Introduction and Prayer for Relief

**Purpose.** Formally petition the court for early release under the medical judicial release framework.

**Authority.** Cite ORC § 2929.20 (judicial release) and ODRC Policy 66-ILL-01 / OCHC Protocol B-35.

**Core assertion.** State that the person's severe medical decline qualifies them as medically incapacitated, terminally ill, or in imminent danger of death, making continued incarceration unnecessary for public safety and contrary to the interests of justice and human dignity.

### II. Procedural History and Sentencing Context

**Convictions.** Detail the guilty pleas — e.g., Robbery (F2), Assault of a Peace Officer (F4), Burglary (F3), Drug Possession (F4), and Attempted Weapons Under Disability (F4).

**Sentencing.** Note that on [Month, Day, Year] the court imposed concurrent sentences yielding a net minimum term of two years and an indefinite maximum of three years under SB 201.

**Current custody.** Confirm the person is housed at [ABC] Correctional Institution.

### III. Medical Mitigation and Factual Grounds

*Requires the specific medical records counsel obtains.*

**Statutory threshold.** Establish that the person meets at least one of the three ODRC definitions (terminally ill, imminent danger of death, or medically incapacitated).

**The CMO certificate.** Attach and heavily cite the certificate, highlighting the CMO's findings on diagnosis, prognosis, ambulatory status, and required care level.

### IV. Legal Argument: Discretion and Public Safety

**Administrative preference for judicial release.** ODRC Policy 66-ILL-01 specifically encourages medical-release decisions by local sentencing courts via OCHC Protocol B-35.

**Addressing the offense-of-violence hurdle.** Acknowledge that administrative "release as if on parole" under ORC § 2967.05 may face scrutiny due to a mandatory sentence for an offense of violence (Robbery F2), but the sentencing court retains ultimate discretion to grant medical judicial release.

**Lack of public threat.** Argue that the person's physical or cognitive deterioration, as verified by the CMO, means they are no longer a threat, and that continuous security supervision provides no additional reduction in escape or harm risk.

### V. Proposed Re-Entry and Aftercare Plan

**Community placement.** Detail where the person will live — e.g., a hospice, specialized nursing facility, or with a named family member/representative.

**Supervision.** Acknowledge that, if granted, the person will be supervised by the Adult Parole Authority under community-control sanctions and will comply with all conditions imposed by the court and APA.

### VI. Conclusion

- Reiterate the request for an expedited hearing given the time-sensitive nature of the declining health.
- Request that the court grant the medical judicial release so the person can receive appropriate care in the community.

> **Practice pointer**
> The motion is only as strong as its evidentiary anchor. Counsel's next strategic step is a formal, firm-letterhead request to the HCA to prompt the CMO into issuing the certificate before the motion is finalized.

# 7. Community Re-Entry and the Managed Care Transition Plan

> **Plain language**
> Before release, the prison and family build a written plan so the person's medical care continues without a gap — doctors lined up, Medicaid in place, a ride home arranged, and the house ready for someone who needs help with daily activities.

## The Managed Care Transition Plan (MCTP)

Developed by the ODRC Bureau of Medical Operations, the MCTP is a comprehensive framework for incarcerated individuals identified as having complex medical needs. It details the exact post-incarceration follow-up appointments required across three critical areas of care, and it is prepared before the person leaves the facility to ensure a seamless transfer of medical management into the community.

| MCTP component | What it covers |
|---|---|
| Medical services | Scheduled physical-health appointments and continued treatment for the underlying condition. |
| Mental-health services | Behavioral-health appointments and continuity of any psychiatric care. |
| Recovery services | Substance-use and recovery support as part of the continued-care strategy. |

## Supporting re-entry steps

- **Medicaid pre-release enrollment** with the IMPC so community care is funded from day one.
- **Community Linkage Worker (CLW) scheduling** of the first physical and behavioral-health appointments to prevent any lapse in care.
- **Housing and ADL readiness** — a home equipped for the person's daily-living needs and proof of stable housing, which the state weighs heavily.
- **Written transportation plan** documenting exactly how the person travels from prison to home on release day.
- **APA supervision** under court-imposed community-control sanctions once release is granted.

# 8. Fallback Strategies ("Plan B")

If the medical judicial release does not succeed — or while it is pending — several other Ohio mechanisms may reduce time served or support eventual release. These are generally weaker or slower than the judicial medical path, and some are expressly limited.

## Sentence-reduction and credit mechanisms

**Reagan Tokes exceptional-conduct reduction (ORC § 2967.271 / SB 201).** The ODRC Director may recommend that the sentencing court reduce the minimum term — up to 15% — for exceptional conduct, subject to the judge's final approval. In practice the Director has interpreted "exceptional conduct" strictly. There is also a rebuttable presumption that an offender is released at the expiration of the minimum term or presumptive earned-early-release date, unless ODRC holds a hearing to rebut it for bad conduct.

**Completion Credit (HB 49).** A one-time credit for completing approved programs, which can reduce the sentence by up to 10% (capped at 90 days).

**Participation Credit (HB 86).** Productive participation in approved programs can earn 1 to 5 days of credit per month, depending on offense eligibility.

**Bonus Credit.** Successful completion of a second participation/completion program can earn an additional 5 days of bonus credit.

**Transitional Control.** In the final 180 days of confinement, eligible individuals may transfer to a licensed halfway house or approved community residence with electronic monitoring.

> **Key limitation**
>
> **Earned credit and mandatory time do not mix.** Ohio law forbids accumulating earned credit while serving mandatory time, and SB 288 raised the overall earned-credit cap to 15% but did not change that bar. The
>
> **Treatment Transfer Program** (up to 365 days in a community treatment facility) is limited to non-violent F3, F4, and F5 offenses and is unavailable until mandatory time is fully served.

## Executive clemency (commutation of sentence)

If standard legal avenues are exhausted, the offender may petition the Ohio Parole Board for executive clemency and seek a commutation — an act of mercy in which the Governor substitutes a lesser punishment. Clemency is entirely discretionary and rarely granted, but severe (though not quite terminal) medical hardship coupled with strong community support can be a compelling mitigation.

> **Note — this is a different track**
>
> The transparency reforms below — public livestreaming of full-board hearings, the right to participate before the full board, volunteer "navigators," pre-hearing staff feedback, and victim access to the ISR — attach to:
>
> **Parole Board** proceedings on the clemency/parole track. They do not control the judicial medical release path in Sections 1–7, where the...
>
> **Sentencing judge** is the decision-maker and the hearing occurs in the Court of Common Pleas. Keep the two tracks distinct when advising a client.

# 9. Attorney–Client Access and Inmate Legal Rights

Because medical petitions are time-sensitive, consistent and confidential access to the incarcerated person is critical. ODRC must facilitate protected access to counsel and legal materials.

## Confidential communication

**Visitation.** Under OAC 5120-9-20, attorney requests for visiting time beyond regular hours "shall be liberally granted" when sufficient reason is shown. ODRC Policy 59-LEG-01 guarantees attorney visits in a private room (visual observation only; aural observation prohibited).

**Legal mail.** Policy 75-MAL-03 governs uncensored written correspondence between the incarcerated person and the legal team.

**Telephone access.** Secure lines for confidential attorney-client conferences, including special unmonitored conferences where the medical condition makes time of the essence.

**Bedside visits.** If the person's condition deteriorates to imminent death and they are moved to hospice or a hospital, ODRC policy allows supervised bedside visits.

## Research, materials, and indigent status

**Law library access.** Electronic access to the Ohio Revised Code, Administrative Code, and published U.S. Supreme Court and Ohio decisions.

**Clerk assistance.** Clerks assist with typing, reading, and drafting initial pleadings for a person filing pro se.

**Materials organization.** Every case document must carry the correct case number, and materials must stay within the 2.4 cubic feet property limit under OAC 5120-9-33.

**Indigent verification.** The librarian or designated staff must confirm indigent status with the Cashier's Office before issuing a legal kit.

**Indigent legal kit contents (Appendix B standard)**

- Two large manila envelopes (10 in × 15 in).
- One black-ink pen.
- One white writing-paper tablet (8.5 in × 11 in).
- Forty sheets of white bond or copy paper.
- Five sheets of carbon paper or a copy card for twenty free copies.

PART II

# The Toolkit: Templates & Worksheets

*Fill-in tools to build and track a real petition, step by step.*

# The First Seven Days

If a loved one in an Ohio prison has become gravely ill, the first week matters. Here is where to put your energy while you arrange counsel.

- ☐ Write down the basics: the person's full name, inmate number, institution, and sentencing county (Worksheet 1).
- ☐ Contact a licensed Ohio attorney about a medical judicial release petition.
- ☐ Ask the institution's Health Care Administrator, in writing, to begin a medical-release evaluation (use the sample letter).
- ☐ Begin gathering identity and medical documents (Worksheet 2).
- ☐ Identify where the person could live and receive care, and who would provide it.
- ☐ Do not contact any witness or alleged victim — ever.

*Keep everything in one binder with this workbook. Bring it to every meeting.*

# Phase Timeline at a Glance

A one-page map of the whole process. Use it to see where a matter stands.

| Phase | What happens | Who leads |
|---|---|---|
| 1. Retention | Hire counsel; sign agreement; gather documents. | Client / caregiver & attorney |
| 2. Medical certification | HCA initiates Protocol B-35; CMO issues certificate. | HCA & Chief Medical Officer |
| 3. Re-entry planning | Medicaid, MCTP, housing, transportation. | Client, IMPC, CLW, caregiver |
| 4. ODRC investigation | Legal clearance, placement investigation, Director's recommendation. | ODRC Legal, DPCS, Director |
| 5. Judicial proceedings | Motion filed; notifications; hearing; decision. | Counsel, prosecutor, judge |

# Sample Motion for Medical Judicial Release

> **How to use this model**
>
> This is a model only. Replace every bracketed field with your facts, confirm each citation against current law, and adapt the argument to the case. Attach the CMO certificate, the Director's recommendation, and the re-entry plan as exhibits.

**IN THE COURT OF COMMON PLEAS**
**[ ABC ] COUNTY, OHIO**

| | |
|---|---|
| STATE OF OHIO, Plaintiff, v.<br>[ INCARCERATED PERSON ],<br>Defendant. | Case No. [ Docket # ] Judge [ First and Last Name ] DEFENDANT'S MOTION FOR A JUDICIAL ORDER OF EARLY RELEASE ON GROUNDS OF MEDICAL NECESSITY |

Now comes the Defendant, by and through undersigned counsel, and respectfully moves this Court for an order granting early release from incarceration on grounds of medical necessity, and for an expedited hearing given the time-sensitive nature of the Defendant's declining health. The grounds for this Motion are set forth below.

### I. Introduction and Prayer for Relief

The Defendant petitions this Court for early release under the medical judicial release framework, R.C. 2929.20 and ODRC Policy 66-ILL-01 (OCHC Protocol B-35). The Defendant's severe and documented medical decline qualifies the Defendant as medically incapacitated, terminally ill, or in imminent danger of death, such that continued incarceration is no longer necessary for public safety and is contrary to the interests of justice and basic human dignity.

### II. Procedural History and Sentencing Context

On [ Month, Day, Year ], following guilty pleas to [ list offenses and degrees ], this Court imposed [ describe sentence, including any mandatory term and the indefinite maximum under S.B. 201 ]. The Defendant is currently housed at [ ABC ] Correctional Institution, Inmate No. [ Inmate # ].

### III. Medical Grounds

The attached certificate of the institution's Chief Medical Officer (Exhibit A) establishes that the Defendant satisfies at least one statutory threshold for medical release. The certificate documents the diagnosis, prognosis, ambulatory status, and the minimum level of community medical care the Defendant now requires. [ Summarize the controlling medical findings. ]

### IV. Legal Argument: Discretion and Public Safety

ODRC Policy 66-ILL-01 encourages medical-release determinations by the local sentencing court through OCHC Protocol B-35, and this Court retains ultimate discretion to grant relief. Although administrative "release as if on parole" under R.C. 2967.05 may be unavailable where a mandatory term for an offense of violence is being served, that limitation does not constrain this Court's judicial authority. As verified by the Chief Medical Officer, the Defendant's condition has so diminished the Defendant's capacity that continued secure confinement provides no measurable reduction in any risk to the public.

### V. Proposed Re-Entry and Aftercare Plan

If released, the Defendant will reside at [ identify hospice, nursing facility, or named caregiver and address ] and will receive continuing care under the attached Managed Care Transition Plan (Exhibit C). The Defendant will be supervised by the Adult Parole Authority and will comply with all community-control sanctions imposed by this Court.

### VI. Conclusion

For the foregoing reasons, the Defendant respectfully requests that this Court set an expedited hearing and enter an order granting medical judicial release so that the Defendant may receive appropriate care in the community.

Respectfully submitted,

______________________________

[ Attorney Name ], Esq. (#[ Bar No. ])
Counsel for Defendant · [ Firm, Address, Phone, Email ]

### Certificate of Service

I certify that a copy of the foregoing was served upon the [ ABC ] County Prosecuting Attorney and all required parties by [ method ] on [ Month, Day, Year ].

# Sample Proposed Order Granting Medical Judicial Release

---

*File a proposed order with the motion so the court can sign without delay. Adapt to local practice and to the conditions the court sets.*

**IN THE COURT OF COMMON PLEAS**
**[ ABC ] COUNTY, OHIO**

| | |
|---|---|
| STATE OF OHIO, Plaintiff, v. [ INCARCERATED PERSON ], Defendant. | Case No. [ Docket # ] Judge [ First and Last Name ] ORDER GRANTING EARLY RELEASE ON GROUNDS OF MEDICAL NECESSITY |

This matter came before the Court on the Defendant's Motion for a Judicial Order of Early Release on Grounds of Medical Necessity. The Court, having reviewed the motion, the certificate of the institution's Chief Medical Officer, the recommendation of the Director of the Department of Rehabilitation and Correction, the proposed Managed Care Transition Plan, and any response, and having considered the interests of justice and public safety, FINDS the motion well taken.

**IT IS THEREFORE ORDERED that:**

- The Defendant is granted early release from incarceration on grounds of medical necessity, effective [ date ].
- The Defendant shall reside at [ placement ] and receive continuing care under the attached Managed Care Transition Plan.
- The Defendant shall be supervised by the Adult Parole Authority under the following community-control sanctions: [ list ].
- The Department shall coordinate transfer and release logistics on the effective date.

**IT IS SO ORDERED.**

______________________________ Date: ____________

Judge [ First and Last Name ], Court of Common Pleas

# Sample Certificate Request Letter to the Health Care Administrator

---

*Place on firm letterhead. This letter formally asks the facility Health Care Administrator (HCA) to initiate a medical-release evaluation under OCHC Protocol B-35. It is often the single step that moves a stalled matter forward.*

[ Date ]

Health Care Administrator [ ABC ] Correctional Institution [ Facility Address ]

**Re: Request to Initiate Medical Release Evaluation — [ Incarcerated Person ], Inmate No. [ Inmate # ]**

Dear Health Care Administrator:

I represent [ Incarcerated Person ], who is in your facility's care. Based on [ his/her/their ] current condition, I respectfully request that the institution initiate a medical release evaluation under OCHC Protocol B-35 and ODRC Policy 66-ILL-01, including a timely assessment by the Chief Medical Officer of whether [ he/she/they ] is terminally ill, in imminent danger of death, or medically incapacitated.

Given the time-sensitive nature of the condition, I ask that the completed certificate be forwarded to ODRC Legal Services as soon as practicable, and that my office be advised of the evaluation's status. I am available to provide records or releases needed to support the evaluation. Thank you for your attention to this urgent matter.

Respectfully,

[ Attorney Name ], Esq. · Counsel for [ Incarcerated Person ]

## Sample Authorization for Release of Medical Records

*Have the incarcerated person sign this so providers and the institution may release records to counsel. Adapt to any provider-specific HIPAA form.*

**I, [ Incarcerated Person ], Inmate No. [ Inmate # ], authorize:**

**(Provider / institution / records custodian):**

**to release my medical and treatment records to:**

**(Attorney / firm):**

Purpose: to support a petition for medical judicial release. This authorization covers diagnoses, prognoses, treatment notes, imaging, and related records. It expires one year from signature unless revoked in writing.

Signature: ______________________________ Date: ________________

# Sample Records Request to a Provider or Facility

*Place on firm letterhead and attach the signed authorization above.*

[ Date ]

Records Custodian [ Provider / Facility ] [ Address ]

**Re: Request for Medical Records — [ Incarcerated Person ], DOB [ date ], Inmate No. [ Inmate # ]**

Dear Records Custodian:

I represent [ Incarcerated Person ] in a time-sensitive matter. Enclosed is a signed authorization. Please provide a complete copy of all medical records in your custody — including diagnoses, prognoses, treatment and progress notes, and imaging — at your earliest convenience. Given the urgency, expedited handling is appreciated. Please advise of any fees in advance.

Thank you for your prompt attention.

Respectfully, [ Attorney Name ], Esq.

## Worksheet 1: Case Intake and Representation

*Capture the essentials at the first meeting.*

**Incarcerated person (full legal name):**

**Inmate number:**

**Institution and location:**

**Sentencing county / Court of Common Pleas:**

**Case / docket number(s):**

**Sentencing judge:**

**Offenses and degrees:**

**Mandatory term? (Y/N) and length:**

**Admission date / projected release date:**

**Primary caregiver / community contact:**

**Representation agreement signed? (date):**

**No-contact reminder:** the incarcerated person and the caregiver must not contact any witness or alleged victim under any circumstances.

## Worksheet 2: Records and Documents Collection

*Track what you have requested and received.*

| Document | Requested (date) | Received (date) |
|---|---|---|
| | | |
| | | |
| | | |
| | | |
| | | |
| | | |
| | | |
| | | |
| | | |
| | | |
| | | |
| | | |
| | | |
| | | |

## Worksheet 3: Medical Threshold Eligibility

*Identify which statutory threshold the evidence supports.*

- ☐ Terminally ill — irreversible, incurable condition likely to cause death within twelve months.
- ☐ Imminent danger of death — reasonably low probability of survival beyond six months.
- ☐ Medically incapacitated — unable to complete activities of daily living without continuous medical care.

**Primary diagnosis:**

**Prognosis / survival estimate:**

**Ambulatory status and ADL limitations:**

**Minimum community care required:**

**Supporting records on hand:**

## Worksheet 4: Five-Phase Progress Tracker

*Mark each phase's status and the date completed.*

| Phase / key step | Owner | Status | Date |
|---|---|---|---|

## Worksheet 5: Stakeholder Contact Log

*Keep every contact in one place.*

| Name | Role | Phone / Email | Notes |
|---|---|---|---|
| | | | |
| | | | |
| | | | |
| | | | |
| | | | |
| | | | |
| | | | |
| | | | |
| | | | |
| | | | |
| | | | |
| | | | |
| | | | |
| | | | |

## Worksheet 6: Community Re-Entry & MCTP Planning

*Build the plan the state will scrutinize.*

**Proposed residence (type and address):**

**Home equipped for ADLs? describe:**

**Medicaid pre-release enrollment status (IMPC):**

**First medical appointment (provider / date):**

**First behavioral-health appointment (provider / date):**

**Recovery / substance-use supports:**

**Transportation plan for release day:**

**Community Linkage Worker (name / contact):**

## Worksheet 7: Evidence and Exhibit Index

*Index every exhibit attached to the motion.*

| Exhibit | Description | Source | Attached? |
|---|---|---|---|
| | | | |
| | | | |
| | | | |
| | | | |
| | | | |
| | | | |
| | | | |
| | | | |
| | | | |
| | | | |
| | | | |
| | | | |

## Worksheet 8: Hearing Preparation Checklist

*Confirm before the hearing.*

- ☐ Motion filed with CMO certificate, Director's recommendation, and re-entry plan attached.
- ☐ Expedited-hearing request made and on the docket.
- ☐ Victim notification confirmed handled by court / prosecutor.
- ☐ Anticipated objections identified and responses prepared.
- ☐ Medical witness or affidavit available if needed.
- ☐ Caregiver prepared to confirm placement and care.
- ☐ Proposed order drafted for the Court.
- ☐ Transportation and intake-on-release logistics ready.

## Worksheet 9: Fallback Strategy Decision Guide

*If the judicial path stalls, weigh these alternatives.*

| Option | Eligible? (Y/N) | Notes / next step |
|---|---|---|
| | | |
| | | |
| | | |
| | | |
| | | |

**Options to weigh:** exceptional-conduct reduction (R.C. 2967.271); earned credit (HB 49 / HB 86 / bonus); transitional control; executive clemency. Remember: earned credit does not accrue during mandatory time.

## Worksheet 10: Cost & Logistics Planner

*Plan the practical and financial side of release day and ongoing care.*

| Item / cost | Who is responsible | Estimate | Set? |
| --- | --- | --- | --- |
| | | | |
| | | | |
| | | | |
| | | | |
| | | | |
| | | | |
| | | | |
| | | | |
| | | | |
| | | | |
| | | | |
| | | | |

## Care & Placement Readiness

*The state scrutinizes where the person will live and how care will continue. Confirm each item.*

- ☐ Residence identified, with a named caregiver or facility and address.
- ☐ Home or facility equipped for the person’s mobility and daily-living needs.
- ☐ Primary medical provider identified; first appointment targeted within days of release.
- ☐ Behavioral-health and recovery supports lined up, if needed.
- ☐ Medicaid pre-release enrollment underway with the IMPC.
- ☐ Medication supply and prescriptions arranged for the transition.
- ☐ Transportation arranged for release day and the first appointments.
- ☐ Caregiver available and willing to confirm the plan to the court.

## What Goes in Your Case Binder

*Keep everything in one place, in this order, and bring it to every meeting.*

- ☐ This workbook, with the worksheets filled in as you go.
- ☐ Identity details: full name, inmate number, institution, sentencing county.
- ☐ Representation agreement and attorney contact information.
- ☐ Medical records and the signed records-release authorization.
- ☐ The Chief Medical Officer's certificate (once issued).
- ☐ Correspondence with the Health Care Administrator and ODRC Legal Services.
- ☐ The Managed Care Transition Plan and re-entry documents.
- ☐ The Director's recommendation and any investigation materials.
- ☐ The filed motion, its exhibits, and the proposed order.
- ☐ Your stakeholder contact log and meeting notes.

## Questions to Ask Your Attorney

*Use these at your first meeting and as the matter develops. Write the answers on the lines.*

- Does my loved one's condition appear to meet one of the three medical thresholds?
- Is there a mandatory term, and how does it affect our options and timing?
- What will you do to get the Chief Medical Officer's evaluation started?
- What is a realistic timeline, and where are the likely delays?
- What can our family do to help — records, placement, the re-entry plan?
- How will victim notification and any objections be handled?
- What are our fallback options if the judicial path stalls?
- What are your fees, and what do they cover?

## Phase 1 — Retention & Initiation

*Check off as completed; use the lines for dates, names, and notes.*

- ☐ Representation agreement signed for the medical-necessity motion.
- ☐ No-contact rule confirmed with client and caregiver.
- ☐ Identity, medical, and housing documents requested.

## Phase 2 — Medical Certification

*Check off as completed; use the lines for dates, names, and notes.*

- ☐ Written request sent to the Health Care Administrator (Protocol B-35).
- ☐ CMO evaluation completed.
- ☐ CMO certificate issued and routed to ODRC Legal Services.

## Phase 3 — Community Re-Entry Planning

*Check off as completed; use the lines for dates, names, and notes.*

- ☐ Medicaid pre-release enrollment started with the IMPC.
- ☐ MCTP appointments scheduled with the Community Linkage Worker.
- ☐ Housing/ADL readiness and transportation plan documented.

## Phase 4 — ODRC Investigation & Director Approval

*Check off as completed; use the lines for dates, names, and notes.*

- ☐ ODRC Legal Services clearance obtained.
- ☐ Placement Investigation Request completed; ISR obtained.
- ☐ Director's recommendation secured and sent to the court.

## Phase 5 — Judicial Proceedings

*Check off as completed; use the lines for dates, names, and notes.*

- ☐ Motion filed with all exhibits attached.
- ☐ Expedited hearing requested; victim notification confirmed.
- ☐ If granted, APA supervision and transfer logistics arranged.

# Motion Drafting Pages

*Use these lines to draft the facts, argument, and proposed order before assembling the motion.*

# Meeting & Call Notes

*Record dates, who you spoke with, and next steps for every contact in the process.*

PART III

# Reference & Support

*Plain-language definitions, common questions, and where to find help.*

# Glossary of Key Terms

| Term | What it means |
|---|---|
| ADLs (Activities of Daily Living) | Basic self-care tasks (eating, bathing, dressing, mobility). An inability to perform them without continuous care supports "medically incapacitated." |
| APA (Adult Parole Authority) | The ODRC unit that supervises people released into the community under court-imposed sanctions. |
| CMO (Chief Medical Officer) | The institution physician who issues the medical certificate that anchors the petition. |
| DPCS (Division of Parole and Community Services) | The ODRC division that investigates the proposed community placement and gathers court, prosecutor, and victim input. |
| HCA (Health Care Administrator) | The facility official who initiates the medical-release evaluation under OCHC Protocol B-35. |
| IMPC (Institution Medicaid Program Coordinator) | Staff who help enroll a person in Medicaid before release so community care is funded. |
| ISR (Institutional Summary Report) | The Warden's report on conduct and rehabilitation, included in the investigation file. |
| CLW (Community Linkage Worker) | Schedules the first community medical and behavioral-health appointments to prevent a lapse in care. |
| MCTP (Managed Care Transition Plan) | The pre-release plan detailing medical, mental-health, and recovery follow-up in the community. |
| OCHC (Office of Correctional Health Care) | The ODRC office whose Protocol B-35 governs the medical release evaluation. |
| ODRC | Ohio Department of Rehabilitation and Correction — the agency that runs Ohio's adult prisons. |
| OVS (Office of Victim Services) | Notifies victims and channels their statements into the process. |
| PIR (Placement Investigation Request) | The DPCS investigation of the proposed home and placement. |
| Judicial release (R.C. 2929.20) | The statute used to ask the sentencing court for early release. |
| Release as if on parole (R.C. 2967.05) | An administrative medical-release route, often barred during mandatory time for an offense of violence. |
| Reagan Tokes Law (S.B. 201 / R.C. 2967.271) | Sets indefinite sentencing, presumptive release at the minimum term, and a Director's exceptional-conduct reduction. |
| Mandatory term | A portion of a sentence that must be served in full; earned credit does not accrue against it. |
| Offense of violence | A statutory category that restricts certain administrative release |

| Term | What it means |
|---|---|
| | routes. |
| Transitional control | Placement in a halfway house or approved residence in the final 180 days of confinement. |
| Commutation / clemency | A discretionary act of mercy by which the Governor substitutes a lesser punishment. |

# Frequently Asked Questions

### Who actually decides whether the person is released?

On the judicial path, the sentencing judge decides. The prison and the ODRC Director investigate and recommend, but the final order comes from the court.

### How sick does the person have to be?

They must meet one of three thresholds certified by the prison's Chief Medical Officer: terminally ill, in imminent danger of death, or medically incapacitated (unable to manage daily living without continuous care).

### A mandatory sentence for a violent offense — is release impossible?

Not necessarily. A mandatory violent-offense term often blocks the administrative route, but the sentencing judge still has discretion to grant medical judicial release. The medical evidence has to be strong.

### What is the single most important document?

The Chief Medical Officer's certificate. Nothing moves without it, which is why families and counsel should press the Health Care Administrator to initiate the evaluation in writing.

### How long does it take?

It varies by facility and court. Because these matters are time-sensitive, counsel should request expedited handling at every stage — from the certificate to the hearing.

### What happens after release is granted?

The person is transferred into the caregiver's care and supervised by the Adult Parole Authority under conditions the court sets. Care continues under the Managed Care Transition Plan.

### Can the victim object?

Yes. The court and prosecutor notify victims, who may submit statements or testimony. Anticipate objections and address them directly.

### Do we need a lawyer?

This is a court proceeding with strict requirements and real stakes. A licensed Ohio attorney should handle the petition; this workbook helps everyone prepare and organize.

### What if the judicial path doesn't work?

Fallback options include exceptional-conduct reduction, earned-credit programs, transitional control, and executive clemency — each with its own limits (see Worksheet 9 and Section 8).

# Resources and Where to Find Help

*Verify current contact details before relying on any resource; agencies and programs change. Use official .gov sources where possible.*

## State agencies

- **Ohio Department of Rehabilitation and Correction (ODRC)** — institution health care, the Office of Correctional Health Care, and the Division of Parole and Community Services. Official site: [ drc.ohio.gov ].
- **Ohio Adult Parole Authority** — post-release supervision. [ contact via ODRC ].
- **Ohio Department of Medicaid** — pre-release enrollment and community coverage. [ medicaid.ohio.gov ].

## Legal help

- **Ohio State Bar Association lawyer referral** — to find Ohio counsel. [ ohiobar.org ].
- **Local legal aid / public defender** — for indigent assistance. [ add county-specific contact ].

## Support and records

- **Institution Health Care Administrator** — first point of contact for the medical evaluation. [ facility phone ].
- **Office of Victim Services** — victim notification and statements. [ via ODRC ].

**Family note:** keep a single binder with this workbook, the records you gather, and your contact log. Bring it to every meeting with counsel.

# Appendix A — Key Authorities Quick-Reference

| Authority | Subject | Practical significance |
|---|---|---|
| ORC § 2929.20 | Judicial release | Statutory vehicle for the early-release motion before the sentencing court. |
| ORC § 2967.05 | Medical release as if on parole | Administrative path generally barred during mandatory time for an offense of violence. |
| ORC § 2967.271 (SB 201) | Reagan Tokes Law | Presumptive release at minimum term; Director's exceptional-conduct reduction (up to 15%). |
| ODRC Policy 66-ILL-01 | Medical-release thresholds | Defines terminal / imminent-danger / incapacitated; encourages judicial decision. |
| OCHC Protocol B-35 | Medical judicial release | Facility-level protocol initiating the medical release evaluation. |
| OAC 5120-9-17 | Eligibility confirmation | Used by ODRC Legal Services to confirm medical-release eligibility. |
| OAC 5120-9-20 | Attorney visitation | Additional attorney visiting time "shall be liberally granted." |
| OAC 5120-9-33 | Legal property limit | Caps legal materials at 2.4 cubic feet. |
| ODRC Policy 59-LEG-01 | Confidential visits | Private-room attorney visits; aural observation prohibited. |
| ODRC Policy 75-MAL-03 | Legal mail | Uncensored attorney-client correspondence. |
| HB 49 / HB 86 / SB 288 | Earned credit | Completion, participation, and bonus credit; 15% cap; no accrual on mandatory time. |
| State v. Clinkscale | Mandatory time & waiting period | Mandatory term must be fully served before any judicial-release waiting period begins; jail-time credit cannot shorten it. |

*Verify each authority against the current official source before relying on it.*

# Appendix B — Template Field Glossary

Replace each placeholder with matter-specific information before using any part of this playbook in an actual filing.

| Placeholder | Supply |
|---|---|
| Incarcerated Person | The client's full legal name. |
| [Inmate #] | ODRC institution number. |
| ABC Correctional Institution | The actual facility name and location. |
| ABC County | The sentencing county / Court of Common Pleas. |
| Neighboring County | Any additional sentencing county and docket. |
| [Docket #] | Case and docket numbers for each matter. |
| [Month, Day, Year] | Admission, sentencing, and projected release dates. |
| [Judge First and Last Name] | The sentencing judge. |
| Client supporter / representative | The named family member or caregiver providing community placement. |

# Appendix C — Master Checklist

*A one-page run of the whole sequence. See the cross-referenced section for detail.*

### Phase 1 — Retention

- ☐ Signed representation agreement specific to the medical-necessity motion (§3).
- ☐ No-contact rules confirmed with client and supporter (§3).
- ☐ Identity and medical/housing documents collected (§3, §5).

### Phase 2 — Medical certification

- ☐ Written request to HCA to initiate OCHC Protocol B-35 (§3, §6).
- ☐ CMO certificate issued and routed to ODRC Legal Services (§2, §5).

### Phase 3 — Re-entry planning

- ☐ Pre-release Medicaid enrollment with IMPC (§7).
- ☐ MCTP built with CLW; transportation and housing/ADL documented (§7).

### Phase 4 — Administrative review

- ☐ ODRC Legal clearance; DPCS placement investigation (§3).
- ☐ Warden's ISR obtained; Director's recommendation secured (§4, §5).

### Phase 5 — Judicial proceedings

- ☐ Motion filed with CMO certificate, Director's recommendation, and re-entry plan (§6).
- ☐ Expedited hearing requested; opposition anticipated (§6).
- ☐ If granted: transfer to supporter's care under APA supervision (§3, §7).

## Notes Pages

*End of workbook.*

**PROFESSOR OWLIE**

*Lessons & Wisdom*

---

---

**Second Ohio Legal Publishing Company**

A division of LegalOwl216 LLC · Cleveland, Ohio

*Plain-language legal guidance for the people who need it — and the professionals who serve them.*

First Edition · June 2026

www.ingramcontent.com/pod-product-compliance
Lightning Source LLC
LaVergne TN
LVHW060043210926
848481LV00013B/3946